WEST COUNTRY POEMS OF WORDSWOF

Illustrated and
Selected by
Richard J. Hutchii

CW00408330

CONTENTS

*   *   *

ILLUSTRATIONS

*   *   *

ISBN 0 9504736 4 2

PREFACE

This selection of the West Country poems of William Wordsworth and Samuel Taylor Coleridge is a companion volume to *The Wordsworth Poetical Guide to the Lakes*. Included here are short biographies of the poets. Many of the poems selected were in the first edition of the *Lyrical Ballads* (1798), and are prefaced by Wordsworth's recollections of their origins as dictated to Miss Isabella Fenwick in the last decade of his life. Owing to the illness of his sister, Dorothy, and the infirmity of his old age, Miss Fenwick took over the role of amenuensis to the poet.

Coleridge left many valuable essays and studies on the works of Wordsworth and himself incorporated in *Biographia Literaria* (1817). Coleridge did his best work at Nether Stowey, whereas Wordsworth experimented—not always successfully. But the work done at Alfoxden, Holford, was the nursery from which grew, in the Lake District, the flourishing plants of his poetic genius. Much of the credit for Wordsworth's development as a poet must go to Coleridge, who gave him true friendship and the sincere criticism and encouragement of a brilliant poet and scholar. Just as important was the part played by Dorothy Wordsworth whom Coleridge regarded as a woman 'exquisite in mind and heart'.

Throughout this volume individual poems, where dates are known, have been arranged chronologically, and the places of origin and dates are displayed at the head of each poem with the name of the poet represented.

R.J.H.

BRIEF BIOGRAPHIES

William Wordsworth

Born 7 April 1770 at Cockermouth in N.W. Cumbria; educated at Hawkshead Grammar School, 1779-87, and at St. John's College, Cambridge, 1787-91; in France 1791-2; with sister Dorothy at Racedown, Dorset, 1795; they met Coleridge at Bristol; moved to Alfoxden, Holford, Somerset July 1797-July 1798; with Coleridge published the *Lyrical Ballads*, September 1798; moved with Dorothy to Town End, Grasmere, Cumbria, December 1799; married Mary Hutchinson, 1802; moved to Rydal Mount, 1813; appointed Poet Laureate 1843; died 23 April 1850; William, his wife Mary and Dorothy buried at Grasmere churchyard.

Samuel Taylor Coleridge

Born 21 October 1772 at Ottery St. Mary, Devonshire; educated at Christ's Hospital, London, July 1782; and at Jesus College, Cambridge, 1 October 1791-December 1793; served with 15th Dragoons; returned to Cambridge 10 April 1794; met Wordsworth, 1795; married Sara Fricker, 4 October 1795; honeymooned at Clevedon, Somerset; moved to Nether Stowey, 31 December 1796; Wordsworths moved to Alfoxden, Holford, nearby, July 1797; Charles Lamb visited Coleridge 7 July; *The Ancient Mariner* begun 13 November 1797; Wedgwoods offered him annuity for life of £150; with Wordsworths in Germany, September 1798-July 1799; moved with family to Greta Hall, Keswick, Cumbria in July 1800; left Wordsworths and Lake District, 1810; died 25 July 1834 at Highgate.

To S. T. Coleridge by William Wordsworth

When, looking back, thou seest, in clearer view
Than any liveliest sight of yesterday,
That summer, under whose indulgent skies,
Upon smooth Quantock's airy ridge we roved
Unchecked, or loitered 'mid her sylvan coombs,
Thou in bewitching words, with happy heart,
Didst chaunt the vision of that Ancient Man,
The bright-eyed Mariner, and rueful woes
Didst utter of the Lady Christabel;
And I, associate with such labour, steeped
In soft forgetfulness the livelong hours,
Murmuring of him who, joyous hap, was found,
After the perils of his moonlight ride,
Near the loud waterfall; or her who sate
In misery near the miserable Thorn;—
When thou dost to that summer turn thy thoughts,
And hast before thee all which then we were,
To thee, in memory of that happiness,
It will be known, by thee at least, my Friend!
Felt, that the history of Poet's mind
Is labour not unworthy of regard:
To thee the work shall justify itself.

(from *The Prelude*)

*   *   *

To William Wordsworth by S. T. Coleridge

And when—O Friend! my comforter and my guide!
Strong in thyself, and powerful to give strength!—
Thy long sustained Song finally closed,
And thy deep voice had ceased—yet thou thyself
Wert still before my eyes, and round us both
That happy vision of beloved faces—
Scarce conscious, and yet conscious of its close
I sate, my being blended in one thought
(Thought was it? or aspiration? or resolve?)
Absorbed, yet hanging still upon the sound—
And when I rose, I found myself in prayer.

'Charles Lamb has been with me for a week', wrote Coleridge in July 1797. 'He left me Friday morning. The second day after Wordsworth came to me, dear Sara emptied a skillet of boiling milk on my foot, which confined me during the whole of C. Lamb's stay, and still prevents me from all walks longer than a furlong.While Wordsworth, his sister Dorothy and Charles Lamb were out one evening, sitting in the arbour of T. Poole's garden, which communicates with mine, I wrote these lines, with which I am pleased. . . .' They describe his neighbour's garden and the surrounding countryside (Charles Lamb was Coleridge's guest from 7 July to 14 July 1797).

This Lime-Tree Bower, My Prison

Well, they are gone, and here must I remain,
This lime-tree bower my prison! I have lost
Beauties and feelings, such as would have been
Most sweet to my remembrance even when age
Has dimm'd mine eyes to blindness! They, meanwhile,
Friends, whom I never more may meet again,
On springy heath, along the hill-top edge,
Wander in gladness, and wind down, perchance,
To that still roaring dell, of which I told;
The roaring dell, o'erwooded, narrow, deep,
And only speckled by the mid-day sun;
Where its slim trunk the ash from rock to rock
Flings arching like a bridge;—that branchless ash,
Unsunn'd and damp, whose few poor yellow leaves
Ne'er tremble in the gale, yet tremble still,
Fann'd by the waterfall! and there my friends
Behold the dark green file of long lank weeds,
That all at once (a most fantastic sight!)
Still nod and drip beneath the dripping edge
of the blue clay-stone.

                              Now, my friends emerge
Beneath the wide wide Heaven—and view again
The many-steepled tract magnificent
Of hilly fields and meadows, and the sea,
With some fair bark, perhaps, whose sails light up
The slip of smooth clear blue betwixt two Isles
Of purple shadow! Yes! they wander on
In gladness all; but thou, methinks, most glad,
My gentle-hearted Charles! for thou hast pined
And hunger'd after Nature, many a year,
In the great city pent, winning thy way

With sad yet patient soul, through evil and pain
And strange calamity! Ah! slowly sink
Behind the western ridge, thou glorious Sun!
Shine in the slant beams of the sinking orb,
Ye purple heath-flowers! richlier burn, ye clouds!
Live in the yellow light, ye distant groves!
And kindle, thou blue Ocean! So my friend
Struck with deep joy may stand, as I have stood,
Silent with swimming sense; yea, gazing round
On the wide landscape, gaze till all doth seem
Less gross than bodily; and of such hues
As veil the Almighty Spirit, when yet he makes
Spirits perceive his presence.

                     A delight
Comes sudden on my heart, and I am glad
As I myself was there! Nor in this bower,
This little lime-tree bower, have I not mark'd
Much that has sooth'd me. Pale beneath the blaze
Hung the transparent foliage; and I watch'd
Some broad and sunny leaf, and lov'd to see
The shadow of the leaf and stem above
Dappling its sunshine! And that walnut-tree
Was richly ting'd, and a deep radiance lay
Full on the ancient ivy, which usurps
Those fronting elms, and now, with blackest mass
Makes their dark branches gleam a lighter hue
Through the late twilight: and though now the bat
Wheels silent by, and not a swallow twitters,
Yet still the solitary humble-bee
Sings in the bean-flower! Henceforth I shall know
That Nature ne'er deserts the wise and pure;
No plot so narrow, be but Nature there,
No waste so vacant, but may well employ
Each faculty of sense, and keep the heart
Awake to Love and Beauty! and sometimes
'Tis well to be bereft of promis'd good,
That we may lift the soul, and contemplate
With lively joy the joys we cannot share.
My gentle-hearted Charles! when the last rook
Beat its straight path along the dusky air
Homewards, I blest it! deeming its black wing
(Now a dim speck, now vanishing in light)
Had cross'd the mighty Orb's dilated glory,
While thou stood'st gazing; or, when all was still,
Flew creaking o'er thy head, and had a charm
For thee, my gentle-hearted Charles, to whom
No sound is dissonant which tells of Life.

The day was 13 November 1797. Alfoxden lay in shadows beneath the trees, and from the mansion which William and Dorothy had leased, they, and Coleridge, emerged on to the lawn. They began their journey to Lynton and the Valley of the Rocks which was to culminate in the writing of *The Rime of the Ancient Mariner*, giving Coleridge a niche among the immortal poets.

The walking tour to Lynton had begun for very mercenary reasons. As always the poets were short of money; but let Wordsworth himself explain their motives for going:

' . . . As our united funds were very small, we agreed to defray the expense of the tour by writing a poem to be sent to the New Monthly Magazine. Accordingly we set off, and proceeded along the Quantock Hills towards Watchet; and in the course of this walk was planned the poem *The Ancient Mariner*, founded on a dream, as Coleridge said, of his friend Mr. Cruikshank. Much the greatest part of the story was Coleridge's invention, but certain parts I myself suggested; for example some crime was to be committed, which should bring upon the Old Navigator—as Coleridge afterwards delighted to call him—the spectral persecution as a consequence of that crime, and his wanderings.

'I had been reading in Shelvocke's *Voyages*, a day or two before, that while doubling Cape Horn, they frequently saw Albatrosses in that latitude, the largest sort of sea-fowl, some twelve or fourteen feet.

' "Suppose," said I, "you represent him as having killed one of these birds on entering the South Sea, and that the tutelary spirits of these regions take it upon them to avenge the crime."

'The incident was thought fit for the purpose, and adopted accordingly. I also suggested the navigation of the ship by the dead men, but do not recollect that I had anything more to do with the theme of the poem.

'The Gloss with which it was subsequently accompanied,' he added, 'was not thought of by either of us at the time; at least not a hint of it was given to me, and I have no doubt it was a gratuitous afterthought.'

Wordsworth only furnished two lines of the poem,

> And listens like a three year's child:
> The Mariner hath his will.

But, although he was able to help largely with the theme, the composition was left to Coleridge. Generally in his choice of material, Wordsworth by nature was more reflective and earthbound. The subject of course demanded a supernatural flavour, which was characteristic of Coleridge's genius.

And so, on his return to Nether Stowey, Coleridge completed the poem. For several of the descriptive passages, he used the local scene. The *Kirk*, for instance, was the Stowey church, and the *loud bassoon* was suggested by the string band and bassoon which accompanied the congregation in the poet's day.

In 1798, *The Rime of the Ancient Mariner* appeared for the first time in the *Lyrical Ballads*, and the poem that was planned purely for financial reasons, became an important milestone in English romantic poetry.

But Coleridge need not have worried about money, because in this same year, Josiah and Thomas Wedgwood, those great patrons of the Arts, settled on him unconditionally an annuity of £150. The sad fact remains, however, that the poet never again completed anything in verse to equal his Mariner, although *Christabel*, written partly at Nether Stowey, came very near it in merit.

The Rime of the Ancient Mariner

Part I

It is an ancient Mariner,
And he stoppeth one of three.
'By thy long grey beard and glittering eye,
Now wherefore stopp'st thou me?

'The Bridegroom's doors are
   opened wide,
And I am next of kin;
The guests are met, the feast is set:
May'st hear the merry din.'

He holds him with his skinny hand,
'There was a ship,' quoth he.
'Hold off! unhand me, greybeard loon!'
Eftsoons his hand dropt he.

He holds him with his glittering eye—
The Wedding-Guest stood still,
And listens like a three year's child:
The Mariner hath his will.

The Wedding-Guest sat on a stone:
He cannot choose but hear;
And thus spake on that ancient man,
The bright-eyed Mariner.

'The ship was cheered, the
   harbour cleared,
Merrily did we drop
Below the kirk, below the hill,
Below the lighthouse top.

'The Sun came up upon the left,
Out of the sea came he!
And he shone bright, and on the right
Went down into the sea.

'Higher and higher every day,
Till over the mast at noon—'
The Wedding-Guest here beat
   his breast,
For he heard the loud bassoon.

The bride hath paced into the hall,
Red as a rose is she;
Nodding their heads before her goes
The merry minstrelsy.

The Wedding-Guest he beat his breast,
Yet he cannot choose but hear;
And thus spake on that ancient man.
The bright-eyed Mariner:

'And now the Storm-blast came, and he
Was tyrannous and strong:
He struck with his o'ertaking wings,
And chased us south along.

'With sloping masts and dipping prow,
As who pursued with yell and blow
Still treads the shadow of his foe,
And forward bends his head,
The ship drove fast, loud
    roared the blast,
And southward aye we fled.

'And now there came both
    mist and snow,
And it grew wondrous cold:
And ice, mast-high, came floating by,
As green as emerald.

'And through the drifts the snowy cliffs
Did send a dismal sheen:
Nor shapes of men nor beasts we ken—
The ice was all between.

'The ice was here, the ice was there,
The ice was all around:
It cracked and growled, and
    roared and howled,
Like noises in a swound!

'At length did cross an Albatross:
Thorough the fog it came:
As if it had been a Christian soul,
We hailed it in God's name.

'It ate the food it ne'er had eat,
And round and round it flew.
The ice did split with a thunder-fit;
The helmsman steered us through!

'And a good south wind
    sprung up behind;
The Albatross did follow,
And every day, for food or play,
Came to the mariner's hollo!

'In mist or cloud, on mast or shroud,
It perched for vespers nine;
Whiles all the night, through
    fog-smoke white,
Glimmered the white Moon-shine.'

'God save thee, ancient Mariner!
From the fiends, that plague
    thee thus!—
Why look'st thou so?'—
    'With my cross-bow
I shot the Albatross!'

Part II

'The sun now rose upon the right:
Out of the sea came he,
Still hid in mist, and on the left
Went down into the sea.

'And the good south wind
    still blew behind,
But no sweet bird did follow,
Nor any day, for food or play,
Came to the mariner's hollo!

'And I had done a hellish thing,
And it would work 'em woe:
For all averred, I had killed the bird
That made the breeze to blow.
Ah wretch! said they, the birds to slay,
That made the breeze to blow!

Nor dim nor red, like God's own head,
The glorious Sun uprist:
Then all averred I had killed the bird
That brought the fog and mist.
'Twas right, said they, such birds to slay,
That bring the fog and mist.

'The fair breeze blew,
    the white foam flew,
The furrow followed free:
We were the first that ever burst
Into that silent sea.

8

'Down dropt the breeze,
    the sails dropt down,
'Twas sad as sad could be;
And we did speak only to break
The silence of the sea!

'All in a hot and copper sky,
The bloody Sun, at noon,
Right up above the mast did stand,
No bigger than the Moon.

'Day after day, day after day,
We stuck, nor breath nor motion;
As idle as a painted ship
Upon a painted ocean.

'Water, water, every where,
And all the boards did shrink;
Water, water, every where,
Nor any drop to drink.

'The very deep did rot: O Christ!
That ever this should be!
Yea, slimy things did crawl with legs
Upon the slimy sea.

'About, about, in reel and rout
The death-fires danced at night;
The water, like a witch's oils,
Burnt green, and blue and white.

'And some in dreams assured were
Of the Spirit that plagued us so:
Nine fathom deep he had followed us,
From the land of mist and snow.

'And every tongue, through
    utter drought,
Was withered at the root;
We could not speak, no more than if
We had been choked with soot.

'Ah! well a-day! what evil looks
Had I from old and young!
Instead of the cross, the Albatross
About my neck was hung.

Part III

'There passed a weary time. Each throat
Was parched, and glazed each eye.
A weary time! A weary time!
How glazed each weary eye!
When looking westward, I beheld,
A something in the sky.

'At first it seemed a little speck,
And then it seemed a mist;
It moved and moved, and took at last
A certain shape, I wist.

'A speck, a mist, a shape, I wist!
And still it neared and neared:
As if it dodged a water-sprite,
It plunged and tacked and veered.

'With throats unslaked,
    with black lips baked,
We could nor laugh nor wail;
Through utter drought all
    dumb we stood!
I bit my arm, I sucked the blood,
And cried, A sail! a sail!

'With throats unslaked,
    with black lips baked,
Agape they heard me call:
Gramercy! they for joy did grin,
And all at once their breath drew in,
As they were drinking all.

' See! see (I cried) she tacks no more!
Hither to work us weal;
Without a breeze, without a tide,
She steadied with upright keel!

'The western wave was all a-flame:
The day was well-nigh done:
Almost upon the western wave
Rested the broad bright Sun;
When that strange shape drove suddenly
Betwixt us and the Sun.

'And straight the Sun was flecked
     with bars,
(Heaven's Mother send us grace!)
As if through a dungeon-grate he peered,
With broad and burning face.

'Alas! (thought I, and my
     heart beat loud)
How fast she nears and nears!
Are those *her* sails that glance in the
     Sun,
Like restless gossameres?

'Are those *her* ribs through
     which the Sun
Did peer, as through a grate?
And is that Woman all her crew?
Is that a Death! and are there two?
Is Death that woman's mate?

'*Her* lips were red, *her* looks were free,
Her locks were yellow as gold:
Her skin was as white as leprosy,
The Nightmare Life-in-Death was she,
Who thicks man's blood with cold.

'The naked hulk alongside came,
And the twain were casting dice;
"The game is done!
     I've won! I've won!"
Quoth she, and whistles thrice.

'The Sun's rim dips; the stars rush out:
At one stride comes the dark;
With far-heard whisper, o'er the sea,
Off shot the spectre-bark.

'We listened and looked sideways up!
Fear at my heart, as at a cup
My life-blood seemed to sip!
The stars were dim, and thick the night,
The steersman's face by his lamp
     gleamed white;
From the sails the dew did drip—
Till clomb above the eastern bar
The horned Moon, with one bright star
Within the nether tip.

'One after one, by the star-dogged
     Moon,
Too quick for groan or sigh, -
Each turned his face
     with a ghastly pang,
And cursed me with his eye.

'Four times fifty living men
(And I heard nor sigh nor groan),
With heavy thump, a lifeless lump,
They dropped down one by one.

'The souls did from their bodies fly—
They fled to bliss or woe!
And every soul, it passed me by,
Like the whizz of my cross-bow!'

Part IV

'I fear thee, ancient Mariner!
I fear thy skinny hand!
And thou art long, and lank,
     and brown,
As is the ribbed sea-sand.

'I fear thee and thy glittering eye,
And thy skinny hand, so brown.'—
'Fear not, fear not,
     thou Wedding-Guest!
This body dropt not down.

'Alone, alone, all, all alone,
Alone on a wide, wide sea!
And never a saint took pity on
My soul in agony.

'The many men, so beautiful!
And they all dead did lie:
And a thousand thousand slimy things
Lived on; and so did I.

'I looked upon the rotting sea,
And drew my eyes away;
I looked upon the rotting deck,
And there the dead men lay.

'I looked to heaven, and tried to pray;
But or ever a prayer had gusht,
A wicked whisper came, and made
My heart as dry as dust.

'I closed my lids, and kept them close,
And the balls like pulses beat;
For the sky and the sea,
    and the sea and the sky,
Lay like a load on my weary eye,
And the dead were at my feet.

'The cold sweat melted
    from their limbs,
Nor rot nor reek did they:
The look with which they looked on me
Had never passed away.

'An orphan's curse would drag to hell
A spirit from on high;
But oh! more horrible than that
Is the curse in a dead man's eye!
Seven days, seven nights,
    I saw that curse,
And yet I could not die.

'The moving Moon went up the sky,
And no where did abide:
Softly she was going up,
And a star or two beside—

'Her beams bemocked the sultry main,
Like April hoar-frost spread;
But where the ship's huge shadow lay,
The charmed water burnt alway
A still and awful red.

'Beyond the shadow of the ship,
I watched the water-snakes:
They moved in tracks of shining white,
And when they reared, the elfish light
Fell off in hoary flakes.

'Within the shadow of the ship
I watched their rich attire:
Blue, glossy green, and velvet black,
They coiled and swam; and every track
Was a flash of golden fire.

'O happy living things! no tongue
Their beauty might declare:
A spring of love gushed from my heart,
And I blessed them unaware!
Sure my kind saint took pity on me,
And I blessed them unaware.

'The self-same moment, I could pray;
And from my neck so free
The Albatross fell off, and sank
Like lead into the sea.

Part V
'Oh, sleep! it is a gentle thing,
Beloved from pole to pole!
To Mary Queen the praise be given!
She sent the gentle sleep from Heaven,
That slid into my soul.

'The silly buckets on the deck,
That had so long remained,
I dreamt that they were filled with dew;
And when I awoke, it rained.

'My lips were wet, my throat was cold,
My garments all were dank;
Sure I had drunken in my dreams,
And still my body drank.

'I moved, and could not feel my limbs:
I was so light—almost
I thought that I had died in sleep,
And was a blessed ghost.

'And soon I heard a roaring wind:
It did not come anear;
But with its sound it shook the sails,
That were so thin and sere.

'The upper air burst into life!
And a hundred fire-flags sheen,
To and fro they were hurried about!
And to and fro, and in and out,
The wan stars danced between.

'And the coming wind did
    roar more loud,
And the sails did sigh like sedge;
And the rain poured down
    from one black cloud;
The Moon was at its edge.

'The thick black cloud was cleft,
    and still
The Moon was at its side:
Like waters shot from some high crag,
The lightning fell with never a jag,
A river steep and wide.

'The loud wind never reached the ship,
Yet now the ship moved on!
Beneath the lightning and the Moon
The dead men gave a groan.

'They groaned, they stirred, they all
    uprose,
Nor spake, nor moved their eyes;
It had been strange, even in a dream,
To have seen those dead men rise.

'The helmsman steered,
    the ship moved on;
Yet never a breeze up-blew;
The mariners all 'gan work the ropes,
Where they were wont to do:
They raised their limbs
    like lifeless tools—
We were a ghastly crew.

'The body of my brother's son
Stood by me, knee to knee;
The body and I pulled at one rope,
But he said nought to me.'

'I fear thee, ancient Mariner!'
'Be calm, thou Wedding-Guest!
'Twas not those souls that fled in pain,
Which to their corses came again,
But a troop of spirits blest:

'For when it dawned—
    they dropped their arms,
And clustered round the mast;
Sweet sounds rose slowly
    through their mouths,
And from their bodies passed.

'Around, around, flew each sweet
    sound,
Then darted to the Sun;
Slowly the sounds came back again,
Now mixed, now one by one.

'Sometimes a-dropping from the sky
I heard the skylark sing;
Sometimes all little birds that are,
How they seemed to fill the sea and air
With their sweet jargoning!

'And now 'twas like all instruments,
Now like a lonely flute;
And now it is an angel's song,
That makes the heavens be mute.

'It ceased; yet still the sails made on
A pleasant noise till noon,
A noise like of a hidden brook
In the leafy month of June,
That to the sleeping woods all night
Singeth a quiet tune.

'Till noon we quietly sailed on,
Yet never a breeze did breathe:
Slowly and smoothly went the ship,
Moved onwards from beneath.

'Under the keel nine fathoms deep,
From the land of mist and snow,
The spirit slid; and it was he
That made the ship to go.
The sails at noon left off their tune,
And the ship stood still also.

'The Sun, right up above the mast,
Had fixed her to the ocean:
But in a minute she 'gan stir,
With a short uneasy motion—
Backwards and forwards half her length,
With a short uneasy motion.

'Then like a pawing horse let go,
She made a sudden bound:
It flung the blood into my head,
And I fell down in a swound.

'How long in that same fit I lay,
I have not to declare;
But ere my living life returned,
I heard and in my soul discerned
Two voices in the air.

' "Is it he?" quoth one,
    "Is this the man?
By him who died on cross,
With his cruel bow he laid full low
The harmless Albatross.

' "The spirit who bideth by himself
In the land of mist and snow,
He loved the bird that loved the man
Who shot him with his bow".

'The other was a softer voice,
As soft as honey-dew:
Quoth he, "The man hath penance done,
And penance more will do."

Part VI

First Voice
' "But tell me, tell me! speak again
Thy soft response renewing—
What makes that ship drive on so fast?
What is the ocean doing?"

Second Voice
' "Still as a slave before his lord,
The ocean hath no blast;
His great bright eye most silently
Up to the Moon is cast—

' "If he may know which way to go;
For she guides him smooth or grim.
See, brother, see! how graciously
She looketh down on him."

First Voice
' "But why drives on that ship to fast,
Without or wave or wind?"

Second Voice
' "The air is cut away before,
And closes from behind.

' "Fly, brother, fly! more high,
    more high!
Or we shall be belated:
For slow and slow that ship will go,
When the Mariner's trance is abated."

'I woke, and we were sailing on,
As in a gentle weather:
'Twas night, calm night,
    the moon was high;
The dead men stood together.

'All stood together on the deck,
For a charnel-dungeon fitter:
All fixed on me their stony eyes,
That in the Moon did glitter.

'The pang, the curse, with which they
    died,
Had never passed away:
I could not draw my eyes from theirs,
Nor turn them up to pray.

'And now this spell was snapt: once
    more
I viewed the ocean green,
And looked far forth, yet little saw
Of what had else been seen—

'Like one, that on a lonesome road
Doth walk in fear and dread,
And having once turned round
    walks on,
And turns no more his head;
Because he knows a frightful fiend
Doth close behind him tread.

'But soon there breathed a wind on me,
Nor sound nor motion made:
Its path was not upon the sea,
In ripple or in shade.

'It raised my hair, it fanned my cheek
Like a meadow-gale of spring—
It mingled strangely with my fears,
Yet it felt like a welcoming.

'Swiftly, swiftly flew the ship,
Yet she sailed softly too:
Sweetly, sweetly blew the breeze—
On me alone it blew.

'Oh! dream of joy! is this indeed
The light-house top I see?
Is this the hill? is this the kirk?[1]
Is this mine own countree?

'We drifted o'er the harbour-bar,[2]
And I with sobs did pray—
O let me be awake, my God!
Or let me sleep alway.

(1) Refers to North Hill, Minehead, and church on hill.
(2) Minehead harbour, in fact.

'The harbour-bay was clear as glass,
So smoothly it was strewn!
And on the bay the moonlight lay,
And the shadow of the Moon.

'The rock shone bright, the kirk no less,
That stands above the rock:
The moonlight steeped in silentness
The steady weathercock.

'And the bay was white with silent light,
Till rising from the same,
Full many shapes, that shadows were,
In crimson colours came.

'A little distance from the prow
Those crimson shadows were:
I turned my eyes upon the deck—
Oh, Christ! what saw I there!

'Each corse lay flat, lifeless and flat,
And, by the holy rood!
A man all light, a seraph-man,
On every corse there stood.

'This seraph-band each waved his hand:
It was a heavenly sight!
They stood as signals to the land,
Each one a lovely light;

'This seraph-band, each waved his hand,
No voice did they impart—
No voice; but oh! the silence sank
Like music on my heart.

'But soon I heard the dash of oars,
I heard the Pilot's cheer;
My head was turned perforce away,
And I saw a boat appear.

'The Pilot, and the Pilot's boy,
I heard them coming fast:
Dear Lord in Heaven! it was a joy
The dead men could not blast.

'I saw a third—I heard his voice:
It is the Hermit good!
He singeth loud his godly hymns
That he makes in the wood,
He'll shrieve my soul, he'll wash away
The Albatross's blood.

Part VII

'This Hermit good lives in that wood
Which slopes down to the sea.
How loudly his sweet voice he rears!
He loves to talk with marineres
That come from a far countree.

'He kneels at morn, and noon, and eve—
He hath a cushion plump:
It is the moss that wholly hides
The rotted old oak-stump.

'The skiff-boat neared:
    I heard them talk,
"Why, this is strange, I trow!
Where are those lights so many and fair,
That signal made but now?"

' "Strange, by my faith!"
    the Hermit said—
"And they answered not our cheer!
The planks looked warped!
    and see those sails,
How thin they are and sere!
I never saw aught like to them,
Unless perchance it were

' "Brown skeletons of leaves that lag
My forest-brook along:
When the ivy-tod is heavy with snow,
And the owlet whoops to the wolf
    below,
That eats the she-wolf's young."

' "Dear Lord! it hath a fiendish look"—
(The Pilot made reply)
"I am a-feared"—"Push on, push on!"
Said the Hermit cheerily.

'The boat came closer to the ship,
But I nor spake nor stirred;
The boat came close beneath the ship,
And straight a sound was heard.

'Under the water it rumbled on,
Still louder and more dread:
It reached the ship, it split the bay;
The ship went down like lead.

"Stunned by that loud
  and dreadful sound,
Which sky and ocean smote,
Like one that hath been seven days
  drowned,
My body lay afloat;
But swift as dreams, myself I found
Within the Pilot's boat.

'Upon the whirl, where sank the ship,
The boat spun round and round;
And all was still, save that the hill
Was telling of the sound.

'I moved my lips—the Pilot shrieked,
And fell down in a fit;
The holy Hermit raised his eyes,
And prayed where he did sit.

'I took the oars: the Pilot's boy,
Who now doth crazy go,
Laughed loud and long, and all the
  while
His eyes went to and fro.
"Ha! ha!" quoth he, "full plain I see,
The Devil knows how to row."

'And now, all in my own countree,
I stood on the firm land!
The Hermit stepped forth from the boat,
And scarcely he could stand.

' "O shrieve me, shrieve me,
  holy man!"
The Hermit crossed his brow.
"Say quick," quoth he,
  "I bid thee say—
What manner of man art thou?"

'Forthwith this frame of
  mine was wrenched
With a woful agony,
Which forced me to begin my tale;
And then it left me free.

'Since then, at an uncertain hour,
That agony returns;
And till my ghastly tale is told,
This heart within me burns.

'I pass, like night, from land to land;
I have strange power of speech;
That moment that his face I see,
I know the man that must hear me:
To him my tale I teach.

'What loud uproar bursts
  from that door!
The wedding-guests are there;
But in the garden-bower the bride
And bride-maids singing are;
And hark the little vesper bell,
Which biddeth me to prayer!

'O Wedding-Guest! this soul hath been
Alone on a wide wide sea:
So lonely 'twas, that God himself
Scarce seemed there to be.

'O sweeter than the marriage-feast,
'Tis sweeter far to me,
To walk together to the kirk
With a goodly company!—

'To walk together to the kirk,
And all together pray,
While each to his great Father bends,
Old men, and babes, and loving friends,
And youths and maidens gay!

'Farewell, farewell! but this I tell
To thee, thou Wedding-Guest!
He prayeth well, who loveth well
Both man and bird and beast.

'He prayeth best, who loveth best
All things both great and small;
For the dear God who loveth us,
He made and loveth all.'

The Mariner, whose eye is bright,
Whose beard with age is hoar,
Is gone; and now the Wedding-Guest
Turned from the bridegroom's door .

He went like one that hath been stunned,
And is of sense forlorn:
A sadder and a wiser man,
He rose the morrow morn.

As mentioned in the preface, Wordsworth dictated to Miss Isabella Fenwick, his recollections of how the Alfoxden poems originated. *Fenwick Notes:* '1798. Composed on the road between Nether Stowey and Alfoxden, extempore.'

Dorothy Wordsworth's *Journal:* '25 January 1798—Went to Poole's after tea. The sky spread over with one continuous cloud, whitened by the light of the moon, which, though her dim shape was seen, did not throw forth so strong a light as to chequer the earth with shadows. At once the clouds seemed to cleave asunder, and left her in the centre of a black-blue vault.' The poem was written on 25 January 1798, but published 1815. Note that the poet borrows imagery from Dorothy's Journal.

A Night-piece

————————The sky is overcast
With a continuous cloud of texture close,
Heavy and wan, all whitened by the Moon,
Which through that veil is indistinctly seen,
A dull, contracted circle, yielding light
So feebly spread that not a shadow falls,
Chequering the ground—from rock, plant, tree, or tower.
At length a pleasant instantaneous gleam
Startles the pensive traveller while he treads
His lonesome path, with unobserving eye
Bent earthwards; he looks up—the clouds are split
Asunder,—and above his head he sees
The clear Moon, and the glory of the heavens.
There in a black-blue vault she sails along,
Followed by multitudes of stars, that, small
And sharp, and bright, along the dark abyss
Drive as she drives: how fast they wheel away,
Yet vanish not!—the wind is in the tree,
But they are silent;—still they roll along
Immeasurably distant; and the vault,
Built round by those white clouds, enormous clouds,
Still deepens its unfathomable depth.
At length the Vision closes; and the mind,
Not undisturbed by the delight it feels,
Which slowly settles into peaceful calm,
Is left to muse upon the solemn scene.

One night in February of 1798, after all his family had retired to bed, Coleridge sat before the fireplace in the living room of his cottage warming his hands. Outside there was a heavy frost and nothing disturbed the silence except the breathing of his child, David Hartley, asleep in a cot at his side. He gazed at the child lovingly, and as he did so he recollected his own youth, his sweet birth-place at the Vicarage, Ottery St. Mary in Devonshire. And as the images passed before his mind's eye, he began to write the following lines:

Frost at Midnight

The Frost performs its secret ministry,
Unhelped by any wind. The owlet's cry
Came loud—and hark, again! loud as before.
The inmates of my cottage, all at rest,
Have left me to that solitude, which suits
Abstruser musings: save that at my side
My cradled infant slumbers peacefully.
'Tis calm indeed! so calm, that it disturbs
And vexes meditation with its strange
And extreme silentness, Sea, hill and wood,
This populous village! Sea, and hill, and wood,
With all the numberless goings-on of life,
Inaudible as dreams! the thin blue flame
Lies on my low-burnt fire, and quivers not;
Only that film, which fluttered on the grate,
Still flutters there, the sole unquiet thing.
Methinks, its motion in this hush of nature
Gives it dim sympathies with me who live,
Making it a companionable form,
Whose puny flaps and freaks the idling Spirit
By its own moods interprets, every where
Echo or mirror seeking of itself,
And makes a toy of Thought.

But O! how oft,
How oft, at school, with most believing mind,
Presageful, have I gazed upon the bars,
To watch that fluttering *stranger*! and as oft
With unclosed lids, already had I dreamt
Of my sweet birth-place, and the old church-tower, [1]
Whose bells, the poor man's only music, rang
From morn to evening, all the hot Fair-day,
So sweetly, that they stirred and haunted me
With a wild pleasure, falling on mine ear
Most like articulate sounds of things to come!
So gazed I, till the soothing things, I dreamt,
Lulled me to sleep, and sleep prolonged my dreams!
And so I brooded all the following morn,
Awed by the stern preceptor's face, mine eye
Fixed with mock study on my swimming book:
Save if the door half opened, and I snatched
A hasty glance, and still my heart leaped up,
For still I hoped to see the *stranger's* face,
Townsman, or aunt, or sister more beloved,
My play-mate when we both were clothed alike!

Dear Babe, that sleepest cradled by my side,
Whose gentle breathings, heard in this deep calm,
Fill up the interspersed vacancies
And momentary pauses of the thought!
My babe so beautiful! it thrills my heart
With tender gladness, thus to look at thee,
And think that thou shalt learn far other lore,
And in far other scenes! For I was reared
In the great city, pent 'mid cloisters dim,
And saw nought lovely but the sky and stars.
But *thou*, my babe! shalt wander like a breeze
By lakes and sandy shores, beneath the crags
Of ancient mountain, and beneath the clouds,
Which image in their bulk both lakes and shores
And mountain crags: so shalt thou see and hear
The lovely shapes and sounds intelligible
Of that eternal language, which thy God
Utters, who from eternity doth teach
Himself in all, and all things in himself.
Great universal Teacher! he shall mould
Thy spirit, and by giving make it ask.

---

(1) Coleridge's 'sweet birth-place' was the Vicarage, Ottery St. Mary, Devonshire.
A plaque in the church-yard commemorates his birth—21 October 1772.

Coleridge's Cottage, Nether Stowey, Somersetshire
(National Trust).

—*Photo: R. J. Hutchings*

Wordsworth's House, Alfoxden, Holford, Somersetshire.
The name is now changed to Alfoxton Park.

—*Photo: R. J. Hutchings*

Lynmouth Bay and the cliffs below Countisbury Hill (886 feet above sea level), and Foreland Point. It was over this hill that the Wordsworths and Coleridge walked to Lynmouth (foreground) when planning *The Ancient Mariner*. Culbone, where Coleridge wrote *Kubla Khan*, is beyond the hill.

Lynmouth, Devonshire

*Countisbury Hill is to the left. Besides the Wordsworths and Coleridge, Southey, Shelley and Tennyson visited the town.
Lynton and the Valley of the Rocks are nearby.*

—*Photo: R. J. Hutchings*

Holford Village, Somersetshire. The Coomb is straight ahead, and Alfoxden to the right.

—Photo: R. J. Hutchings

Alfoxden from the hill-top (near Holford), whence the Wordsworths and Coleridge set out to walk to Lynton, while planning 'The Ancient Mariner'.

—Photo: R. J. Hutchings

Therefore all seasons shall be sweet to thee,
Whether the summer clothe the general earth
With greenness, or the redbreast sit and sing
Betwixt the tufts of snow on the bare branch
Of mossy apple-tree, while the nigh thatch
Smokes in the sun-thaw; whether the eave-drops fall
Heard only in the trances of the blast,
Or if the secret ministry of frost
Shall hang them up in silent icicles,
Quietly shining to the quiet Moon.

*   *   *

ALFOXDEN,   WORDSWORTH
18 March 1798

A Whirl-Blast From Behind the Hill

Fenwick Notes: 'Observed in the holly grove at Alfoxden, where these verses were written in the spring of 1798' — WW.
Dorothy Wordsworth's *Journal* 18 March 1798: 'The Coleridges left us. A cold, windy morning. Walked with them half way. On our return, sheltered under the hollies, during a hail-shower. The withered leaves danced with the hailstones. William wrote a description of the storm.'
Again Wordsworth borrows imagery from Dorothy's Journal, when describing the withered, dancing leaves.

A whirl-blast from behind the hill
Rushed o'er the wood with startling sound;
Then—all at once the air was still,
And showers of hailstones pattered round.
Where leafless oaks towered high above,
I sat within an undergrove
Of tallest hollies, tall and green;
A fairer bower was never seen.
From year to year the spacious floor
With withered leaves is covered o'er,
And all the year the bower is green.

But see! where'er the hailstones drop
The withered leaves all skip and hop;
There's not a breeze—no breath of air—
Yet here, and there, and every where
Along the floor, beneath the shade
By those embowering hollies made,
The leaves in myriads jump and spring,
As if with pipes and music rare
Some Robin Good-fellow[1] were there,
And all those leaves, in festive glee,
Were dancing to the minstrelsy.

(1) *Robin Goodfellow*—a Puck or hobgoblin (see Shakespeare's *Midsummer Night's Dream* II, i).

19

Lines Written in Early Spring

Wordsworth recalled: 'The brook ran down a sloping rock, so as to make a waterfall, considerable for the county: and across the pool below had fallen a tree—an ash, if I rightly remember—from which rose perpendicularly boughs in search of the light intercepted by the deep shade above. The boughs bore leaves of green, that for want of sunshine had faded into almost lilywhite; and from the underside of this natural sylvan bridge depended long and beautiful tresses of ivy, which waved gently in the breeze, that might, poetically speaking, be called the breath of the waterfall. This motion varied, of course, in proportion to the power of water in the brook. When, with dear friends, I revisited this spot, after an interval of more than forty years, this interesting feature of the scene was gone. To the owner of the place I could not but regret that the beauty of this retired part of the grounds had not tempted him to make it more accessible by a path, not broad or obtrusive, but sufficient for persons who love such scenes to creep along without difficulty.'

I heard a thousand blended notes,
While in a grove I sate reclined,
In that sweet mood when pleasant thoughts
Bring sad thoughts to the mind.

To her fair works did Nature link
The human soul that through me ran;
And much it grieved my heart to think
What man has made of man.

Through primrose tufts, in that green bower,
The periwinkle trailed its wreaths;
And 'tis my faith that every flower
Enjoys the air it breathes.

The birds around me hopped and played,
Their thoughts I cannot measure:—
But the least motion which they made,
It seemed a thrill of pleasure.

The budding twigs spread our their fan,
To catch the breezy air;
And I must think, do all I can,
That there was pleasure there.

If this belief from heaven be sent,
If such be Nature's holy plan,
Have I not reason to lament
What man has made of man?

To My Sister

Fenwick Notes: 'Composed in front of Alfoxden House. My little boy-messenger on this occasion was the son of Basil Montagu. The larch mentioned in the first stanza was standing when I revisited the place, more than forty years after. I was disappointed that it had not improved in appearance as to size, nor had it acquired anything of the majesty of age which, even though less perhaps than any other tree, the larch sometimes does. A few score yards from this tree there grew, when we inhabited Alfoxden, one of the most remarkable beech trees ever seen. The ground sloped both toward and from it. It was of immense size and threw out arms that struck into the soil, like those of the banyan tree, and rose again from it. Two of the branches thus inserted themselves twice, which gave to each the appearance of a serpent moving along by gathering itself up in folds. One of the large boughs of this tree had been torn off by the wind before we left Alfoxden, but five remained. In 1841 we could barely find the spot where the tree had stood. So remarkable a production of Nature could not have been wilfully destroyed'.—WW

To My Sister was written in 1798 and published the same year:

> It is the first mild day of March:
> Each minute sweeter than before,
> The redbreast sings from the tall larch
> That stands beside our door.
>
> There is a blessing in the air,
> Which seems a sense of joy to yield
> To the bare trees, and mountains bare,
> And grass in the green field.
>
> My sister! ('tis a wish of mine)
> Now that our morning meal is done,
> Make haste, your morning task resign;
> Come forth and feel the sun.
>
> Edward will come with you;—and, pray,
> Put on with speed your woodland dress;
> And bring no book; for this one day
> We'll give to idleness.
>
> No joyless forms shall regulate
> Our living calendar:
> We from today, my Friend, will date
> The opening of the year.
>
> Love, now a universal birth,
> From heart to heart is stealing,
> From earth to man, from man to earth:
> —It is the hour of feeling.

One moment now may give us more
Than years of toiling reason:
Our minds shall drink at every pore
The spirit of the season.

Some silent laws our hearts will make,
Which they shall long obey:
We for the year to come may take
Our temper from today.

And from the blessed power that rolls
About, below, above,
We'll frame the measure of our souls:
They shall be tuned to love.

Then come, my Sister! come, I pray,
With speed put on your woodland dress;
And bring no book: for this one day
We'll give to idleness.

*   *   *

ALFOXDEN,   WORDSWORTH
Spring 1798

Anecdote for Fathers,
Showing how the art of lying may be taught

Fenwick Notes: 'This was suggested in front of Alfoxden. The boy
was a son of my friend Basil Montagu, who had been two or three
years under our care. The name Kilve is from a village, where Mr.
Coleridge, my sister, and I had been visiting the famous John Thelwall.
. . . The visit of this man to Coleridge was the occasion of a spy being sent
by Government to watch our proceedings, which were such as the world
would have thought ludicrously harmless'.—WW. Edward Montagu in
fact stayed with the Wordsworths from 1795 until July 1798. The poem was
published 1798.

I have a boy of five years old;
His face is fair and fresh to see;
His limbs are cast in beauty's mould,
And dearly he loves me.

One morn we strolled on our dry walk,
Our quiet home all full in view,
And held such intermitted talk
As we were wont to do.

My thoughts on former pleasures ran;
I thought of Kilve's delightful shore,
Our pleasure home when spring began,
A long, long year before.

22

A day it was when I could bear
Some fond regrets to entertain;
With so much happiness to spare,
I could not feel a pain.

The green earth echoed to the feet
Of lambs that bounded through the glade,
From shade to sunshine, and as fleet
From sunshine back to shade.

Birds warbled round me—and each trace
Of inward sadness had its charm;
Kilve,[1] thought I, was a favoured place,
And so is Liswyn Farm. [2]

My boy beside me tripped, so slim
And graceful in his rustic dress!
And, as we talked, I questioned him,
In very idleness.

'Now tell me, had you rather be,'
I said, and took him by the arm,
'On Kilve's smooth shore, by the green sea,
Or here at Liswyn Farm?'

In careless mood he looked at me,
While still I held him by the arm,
And said, 'At Kilve I'd rather be
Than here at Liswyn Farm.'

'Now, little Edward, say why so:
My little Edward, tell me why.'—
'I cannot tell, I do not know.'—
'Why, this is strange,' said I;

'For here are woods, hills smooth and warm;
There surely must some reason be
Why you would change sweet Liswyn Farm
For Kilve by the green sea.'

At this my boy hung down his head,
He blushed with shame, nor made reply;
And three times to the child I said,
'Why, Edward, tell me why?'

(1) A nearby village on the coast.
(2) Liswyn Farm in the Wye Valley where the poet stayed earlier.

His head he raised—there was in sight,
It caught his eye, he saw it plain—
Upon the house-top, glittering bright,
A broad and gilded vane.

Then did the boy his tongue unlock,
And eased his mind with this reply:
'At Kilve there was no weather-cock;
And that's the reason why.'

O dearest, dearest boy! my heart
For better lore would seldom yearn,
Could I but teach the hundredth part
Of what from thee I learn.

ALFOXDEN   WORDSWORTH
Spring, 1798   *We Are Seven*

We are Seven was written at Alfoxden in the spring of 1798, and the little girl, the heroine, he met within the area of Goodrich Castle in 1793. The lines came to him as he walked in Alfoxden Grove. The last stanza came to him first, having begun with the last line.

'When it was all but finished,' confessed Wordsworth, 'I came in and recited it to Mr. Coleridge and my sister, and said, "A prefatory stanza must be added, and I should sit down to our little tea-meal with greater pleasure if my task was finished." . . . Coleridge immediately threw off the line, thus—   A little child, dear brother Jem.
I objected to the rhyme 'dear brother Jem' as being ludicrous; but we all enjoyed the joke of hitching in our friend James Tobin's name, who was familiarly called Jem.

' He was the brother of the dramatist; and this reminds me of an anecdote which it may be worth while here to notice. The said Jem got sight of the *Lyrical Ballads* as it was going through the press at Bristol. . . .

'One evening he came to me with a grave face and said, "Wordsworth, I have seen the volume that you and Coleridge are about to publish. There is one poem in it I earnestly entreat you will cancel; for, if published, it will make you everlastingly ridiculous. . . . It is called, *We Are Seven*". "Nay," said I, "that shall take its chance however," and he left me in despair.'

—A simple Child,
That lightly draws its breath,
And feels its life in every limb,
What should it know of death?

I met a little cottage Girl:
She was eight years old, she said;
Her hair was thick with many a curl
That clustered round her head.

She had a rustic, woodland air,
And she was wildly clad:
Her eyes were fair, and very fair;
—Her beauty made me glad.

24

'Sisters and brothers, little maid,
How many may you be?'
'How many? Seven in all,' she said,
And wondering looked at me.

'And where are they? I pray you tell.'
She answered, 'Seven are we;
And two of us at Conway dwell,
And two are gone to sea.

'Two of us in the church-yard lie,
My sister and my brother;
And, in the church-yard cottage, I
Dwell near them with my mother.'

'You say that two at Conway dwell,
And two are gone to sea,
Yet ye are seven; I pray you tell
Sweet Maid, how this may be?'

Then did the little Maid reply,
'Seven boys and girls are we;
Two of us in the church-yard lie,
Beneath the church-yard tree.'

'You run about, my little maid,
Your limbs they are alive;
If two are in the church-yard laid,
Then ye are only five.

'Their graves are green, they may be
        seen,'
The little Maid replied,
Twelve steps or more from
        my mother's door,
And they are side by side.

'My stockings there I often knit,
My 'kerchief there I hem;
And there upon the ground I sit,
And sing a song to them.

'And often after sunset, Sir,
When it is light and fair,
I take my little porringer,
And eat my supper there.

'The first that died was sister Jane:
In bed she moaning lay,
Till God released her of her pain,
And then she went away.

'So in the church-yard she was laid;
And, when the grass was dry,
Together round her grave we played,
My brother John and I.

'And when the ground was
    white with snow,
And I could run and slide,
My brother John was forced to go,
And he lies by her side.'

'How many are you, then,' said I,
'If they two are in Heaven?'
Quick was the little Maid's reply,
'O Master! we are seven.'

'But they are dead; those two are dead!
Their spirits are in heaven!'
'Twas throwing words away; for still
The little Maid would have her will,
And said, 'Nay, we are seven!'

ALFOXDEN   WORDSWORTH
19 March 1798

The Thorn (extract)

Fenwick Notes: '*The Thorn* (1798) arose out of my observing, on the ridge
of the Quantock Hill, on a stormy day, a thorn, which I had often passed
in calm and bright weather without noticing it. I said to myself: "Cannot
I by some invention do as much to make this thorn permanently and as
impressive an object as the storm has made it to my eyes at this moment?"
I began the poem accordingly, and composed it with great rapidity. Sir
George Beaumont painted a picture from it, which Wilkie thought his
best. The sky in this picture is nobly done, but it reminds one too much of
Wilson.'—WW.

Dorothy Wordsworth in her *Journal* notes: 19 *March* 1798—'Wm and
Basil and I walked to the hill-tops, a very cold bleak day. We were met on
our return by a severe hailstorm. William wrote some lines describing a
stunted thorn.' 21 *January* 1798: 'Those oaks fanned by the sea breeze,
thick with feathery sea-green moss, as grove not stripped of its leaves.'

1

'There is a Thorn it looks so old,
In truth, you'd find it hard to say,
How it could ever have been young,
It looks so old and grey.
Not higher than a two years' child,
It stands erect this aged Thorn;
No leaves it has, no prickly points;
It is a mass of knotty joints,
A wretched thing forlorn.
It stands erect, and like a stone
With lichens it is overgrown.

26

Like a rock or stone, it is o'ergrown
With lichens to the very top,
And hung with heavy tufts of moss,
A melancholy crop:
Up from the earth these mosses creep,
And this poor Thorn they clasp it round
So close, you'd say that they are bent
With plain and manifest intent,
To drag it to the ground;
And all have joined in one endeavour,
To bury this poor Thorn for ever. . . .

*　　*　　*

ALFOXDEN,   WORDSWORTH
1798

Simon Lee, the Old Huntsman

Fenwick Notes: 'This old man had been huntsman to the squires
of Alfoxden, which, at the time we occupied it, belonged to a minor.
The old man's cottage stood upon the common, a little way from the
entrance to Alfoxden Park. But it had disappeared. Improvements but
rarely appear such to those who, after long intervals of time, revisit
places they have had much pleasure in. The expression when the hounds
were out, "I dearly love their voice," was word for word from his own
lips.'—WW. The poem was written and published in 1798.

In the sweet shire of Cardigan,
Not far from pleasant Ivor-hall,
An old Man dwells, a little man,—
'Tis said he once was tall.
Full five-and-thirty years he lived
A running huntsman merry;
And still the centre of his cheek
Is red as a ripe cherry.

No man like him the horn could sound,
And hill and valley rang with glee
When Echo bandied, round and round,
The halloo of Simon Lee.
In those proud days, he little cared
For husbandry or tillage;
To blither tasks did Simon rouse
The sleepers of the village.

He all the country could outrun,
Could leave both man and horse behind;
And often, ere the chase was done,
He reeled, and was stone-blind.
And still there's something in the world
At which his heart rejoices;
For when the chiming hounds are out,
He dearly loves their voices!

But, oh the heavy change!—bereft
Of health, strength, friends, and kindred, see!
Old Simon to the world is left
In liveried poverty.
His Master's dead,—and no one now
Dwells in the Hall of Ivor;
Men, dogs, and horses, all are dead;
He is the sole survivor.

And he is lean, and he is sick;
His body, dwindled and awry,
Rests upon ankles swoln and thick;
His legs are thin and dry.
One prop he has, and only one,
His wife, an aged woman,
Lives with him, near the waterfall,
Upon the village Common.

Beside their moss-grown hut of clay,
Not twenty paces from the door,
A scrap of land they have, but they
Are poorest of the poor.
This scrap of land he from the heath
Enclosed when he was stronger;
But what to them avails the land
Which he can till no longer?

Oft, working by her Husband's side,
Ruth does what Simon cannot do;
For she, with scanty cause for pride,
Is stouter of the two.
And, though you with your utmost skill
From labour could not wean them,
'Tis little, very little—all
That they can do between them.

Few months of life has he in store
As he to you will tell,
For still, the more he works, the more
Do his weak ankles swell.
My gentle Reader, I perceive
How patiently you've waited,
And now I fear that you expect
Some tale will be related.

O Reader! had you in your mind
Such stores as silent thought can bring,
O gentle Reader! you, would find
A tale in every thing.
What more I have to say is short,
And you must kindly take it:
It is no tale; but, should you think,
Perhaps a tale you'll make it.

One summer-day I chanced to see
This old Man doing all he could
To unearth the root of an old tree,
A stump of rotten wood.
The mattock tottered in his hand;
So vain was his endeavour,
That at the root of the old tree
He might have worked for ever.

'You're overtasked, good Simon Lee,
Give me your tool,' to him I said;
And at the word right gladly ᴸ
Received my proferred aid.
I struck, and with a single blow
The tangled root I severed,
At which the poor old Man so long
And vainly had endeavoured.

The tears into his eyes were brought,
And thanks and praises seemed to run
So fast out of his heart, I thought
They never would have done.
—I've heard of hearts unkind, kind deeds
With coldness still returning;
Alas! the gratitude of men
Hath oftener left me mourning.

It is believed that Coleridge was taken ill on one of his return walks from Lynton to Alfoxden in the spring of 1798, and that he stayed either at Ash Farm or Broomstreet Farm, Culbone, Porlock Hill, until he recovered. In *Biographia Literaria* (1817) he relates that, during his recovery, and after taking laudanum, he experienced a most realistic dream in which the well-known lines of the poem, *Kubla Khan* formed themselves. But he was disturbed by the arrival of a businessman to see him. It was this interruption that distracted him from completing the transcription on to paper of his dream-poem. Though he preserved 54 lines of it, some eight or ten lines escaped his memory.

Kubla Khan [1]

In Xanadu did Kubla Khan
A stately pleasure-dome decree:
Where Alph, the sacred river, ran
Through caverns measureless to man
    Down to a sunless sea.
So twice five miles of fertile ground
With walls and towers were girdled round:
And there were gardens bright with sinuous rills,
Where blossomed many an incense-bearing tree;
And here were forests ancient as the hills,
Enfolding sunny spots of greenery.

But oh! that deep romantic chasm which slanted
Down the green hill athwart a cedarn cover!
A savage place! as holy and enchanted
As e'er beneath a waning moon was haunted
By woman wailing for her demon-lover!
And from this chasm, with ceaseless turmoil seething,
As if this earth in fast thick pants were breathing,
A mighty fountain momently was forced:
Amid whose swift half-intermitted burst
Huge fragments vaulted like rebounding hail,
Or chaffy grain beneath the thresher's flail:
And 'mid these dancing rocks at once and ever
It flung up momently the sacred river.

(1) Cp. *Purchas his Pilgrimage:* 'In Xamdu did Cublai Can build a stately Palace, encompassing sixteene miles of plaine ground with a wall, wherein are fertile Meddowes, pleasant Springs, delightfull Streames, and all sorts of beasts of chase and game, and in the middest thereof a sumptuous house of pleasure' (1626).

Five miles meandering with a mazy motion
Through wood and dale the sacred river ran,
Then reached the caverns measureless to man,
And sank in tumult to a lifeless ocean:
And 'mid this tumult Kubla heard from far
Ancestral voices prophesying war!
　　The shadow of the dome of pleasure
　　Floated midway on the waves;
　　Where was heard the mingled measure
　　From the fountain and the caves.
It was a miracle of rare device,
A sunny pleasure-dome with caves of ice!

　　A damsel with a dulcimer
In a vision once I saw:
It was an Abyssinian maid,
　　And on her dulcimer she played,
　　Singing of Mount Abora.
　　Could I revive within me
　　Her symphony and song,
　　To such a deep delight 'twould win me,
That with music loud and long,
I would build that dome in air,
That sunny dome! those caves of ice!
And all who heard should see them there,
And all should cry, Beware! Beware!
His flashing eyes, his floating hair!
Wave a circle round him thrice,
And close your eyes with holy dread,
For he on honey-dew hath fed,
And drunk the milk of Paradise.

NETHER STOWEY,　　　　　　　　　　　　COLERIDGE
20 April 1798

The lease of Alfoxden to the Wordsworths terminated in July 1798. They had been given, by Mrs. St. Albyn, a three months' notice to quit under suspicion of being spies, although much pleading on their behalf by Coleridge's influential friends at Nether Stowey had been made, they were yet compelled to leave. By April 1798 everybody, including Coleridge, feared a French invasion. He expressed these fears in his poem *Fears in Solitude:* (an extract)

　　　　　　　　　　　　　　　　May my fears,
My filial fears, be vain! and may the vaunts
And menace of the vengeful enemy
Pass like the gust, that roared and died away
In the distant tree: which heard, and only heard
In this low dell, bowed not the delicate grass. . . .

31

And now, beloved Stowey! I behold
Thy church-tower and, methinks, the four huge elms
Clustering, which mark the mansion of my friend;
And close behind them, hidden from my view,
Is my own lowly cottage, where my babe
And my babe's mother dwell in peace! With light
And quickened footsteps thitherward I tend,
Remembering thee, O green and silent dell!
And grateful, that by nature's quietness
And solitary musings, all my heart
Is softened, and made worthy to indulge
Love, and the thoughts that yearn for human kind.

* * *

Dorothy Wordsworth's *Journal*, 20 April 1798: 'Walked in the evening up the hill dividing the Coombs. Came home the Brookham way, by the thorn, and the "Little muddy pond". Nine o'clock at our return. William all the morning engaged in wearisome composition. The moon crescent. *Peter Bell* begun (Coleridge also wrote his *Fears in Solitude* that day).'

Although composed in 1798, *Peter Bell* was not published until 1819 with a dedicatory letter to Robert Southey, Coleridge's brother-in-law. In 1819 Wordsworth was living at Rydal Mount and Southey at Greta Hall, Keswick in the Lake District. While at Racedown and Alfoxden, Wordsworth also wrote 'The Wanderer', which became the first part of *The Excursion* which Keats admired so much. *The Excursion*, also, was not published until Wordsworth was living at Rydal Mount, in the year 1814.

Regrettably, because of their great length, neither of these poems can be included here, but it is appropriate to end with one of the finest poems of this period, *Lines Composed a Few Miles above Tintern Abbey, on Revisiting the Banks of the Wye during a Tour. 13 July*, 1798, a poem which concluded the *Lyrical Ballads*.

WYE VALLEY   WORDSWORTH
13 July 1798

Lines Composed above Tintern Abbey

Five years have past; five summers, with the length
Of five long winters! and again I hear
These waters, rolling from their mountain-springs
With a soft inland murmur.—Once again
Do I behold these steep and lofty cliffs,
That on a wild secluded scene impress
Thoughts of more deep seclusion; and connect
The landscape with the quiet of the sky.

The day is come when I again repose
Here, under this dark sycamore, and view
These plots of cottage-ground, these orchard-tufts,
Which at this season, with their unripe fruits,
Are clad in one green hue, and lose themselves
'Mid groves and copses. Once again I see
These hedgerows, hardly hedgerows, little lines
Of sportive wood run wild: these pastoral farms,
Green to the very door; and wreaths of smoke
Sent up, in silence, from among the trees!
With some uncertain notice, as might seem
Of vagrant dwellers in the houseless woods,
Or of some Hermit's cave, where by his fire
The Hermit sits alone.

                    These beauteous forms,
Through a long absence, have not been to me
As is a landscape to a blind man's eye:
But oft, in lonely rooms, and 'mid the din
Of towns and cities, I have owed to them,
In hours of weariness, sensations sweet,
Felt in the blood, and felt along the heart;
And passing even into my purer mind,
With tranquil restoration:—feelings too
Of unremembered pleasure: such, perhaps,
As have no slight or trivial influence
On that best portion of a good man's life,
His little, nameless, unremembered, acts
Of kindnes and of love. Nor less, I trust,
To them I may have owed another gift,
Of aspect more sublime; that blessed mood,
In which the burthen of the mystery,
In which the heavy and the weary weight
Of all this unintelligible world,
Is lightened:—that serene and blessed mood,
In which the affections gently lead us on,—
Until, the breath of this corporeal frame
And even the motion of our human blood
Almost suspended, we are laid asleep
In body, and become a living soul:
While with an eye made quiet by the power
Of harmony, and the deep power of joy,
We see into the life of things.

                                            If this
Be but a vain belief, yet, oh! how oft—
In darkness and amid the many shapes
Of joyless daylight; when the fretful stir
Unprofitable, and the fever of the world,
Have hung upon the beatings of my heart—
How oft, in spirit, have I turned to thee,
O sylvan Wye! thou wanderer thro' the woods,
How often has my spirit turned to thee!

    And now, with gleams of half-extinguished thought,
With many recognitions dim and faint,
And somewhat of a sad perplexity,
The picture of the mind revives again:
While here I stand, not only with the sense
Of present pleasure, but with pleasing thoughts
That in this moment there is life and food
For future years. And so I dare to hope,
Though changed, no doubt, from what I was when first
I came among these hills; when like a roe
I bounded o'er the mountains, by the sides
of the deep rivers, and the lonely streams,
Wherever nature led: more like a man
Flying from something that he dreads than one
Who wought the thing he loved. For nature then
(The coarser pleasures of my boyish days,
And their glad animal movements all gone by)
To me was all in all.—I cannot paint
What then I was. The sounding cataract
Haunted me like a passion: the tall rock,
The mountain, and the deep and gloomy wood,
Their colours and their forms, were then to me
An appetite; a feeling and a love,
That had no need of a remoter charm,
By thought supplied, nor any interest
Unborrowed from the eye.—That time is past,
And all its aching joys are now no more,
And all its dizzy raptures. Not for this
Faint I, nor mourn nor murmur; other gifts
Have followed; for such loss, I would believe,
Abundant recompense. For I have learned
To look on nature, not as in the hour
Of thoughtless youth; but hearing oftentimes
The still, sad music of humanity,
Nor harsh nor grating, though of ample power
To chasten and subdue. And I have felt
A presence that disturbs me with the joy

Of elevated thoughts; a sense sublime
Of something far more deeply interfused,
Whose dwelling is the light of setting suns,
And the round ocean and the living air,
And the blue sky, and in the mind of man:
A motion and a spirit, that impels
All thinking things, all objects of all thought,
And rolls through all things. Therefore am I still
A lover of the meadows and the woods,
And mountains; and of all that we behold
From this green earth; of all the mighty world
Of eye, and ear,—both what they half create,
And what perceive; well pleased to recognise
In nature and the language of the sense
The anchor of my purest thoughts, the nurse,
The guide, the guardian of my heart, and soul
Of all my moral being.
                              Nor perchance,
If I were not thus taught, should I the more
Suffer my genial spirits to decay:
For thou art with me here upon the banks
Of this fair river; thou my dearest Friend,
My dear, dear Friend; and in thy voice I catch
The language of my former heart, and read
My former pleasures in the shooting lights
Of thy wild eyes. Oh! yet a little while
May I behold in thee what I was once,
My dear, dear Sister! and this prayer I make,
Knowing that Nature never did betray
The heart that loved her; 'tis her privilege,
Through all the years of this our life, to lead
From joy to joy: for she can so inform
The mind that is within us, so impress
With quietness and beauty, and so feed
With lofty thoughts, that neither evil tongues,
Rash judgements, nor the sneers of selfish men,
Nor greetings where no kindness is, nor all
The dreary intercourse of daily life,
Shall e'er prevail against us, or disturb
Our cheerful faith, that all which we behold
Is full of blessings. Therefore let the moon
Shine on thee in thy solitary walk;
And let the misty mountain-winds be free
To blow against thee: and, in after years,
When these wild ecstasies shall be matured
Into a sober pleasure; when thy mind
Shall be a mansion for all lovely forms,
Thy memory be as a dwelling-place
For all sweet sounds and harmonies; oh! then,

If solitude, or fear, or pain, or grief,
Should be thy portion, with what healing thoughts
Of tender joy wilt thou remember me,
And these my exhortations! Nor, perchance—
If I should be where I no more can hear
Thy voice, nor catch from thy wild eyes these gleams
Of past existence—wilt thou then forget
That on the banks of this delightful stream
We stood together; and that I, so long
A worshipper of Nature, hither came
Unwearied in that service: rather say
With warmer love—oh! with far deeper zeal
Of holier love. Nor wilt thou then forget
That after many wanderings, many years
Of absence, these steep woods and lofty cliffs,
And this green pastoral landscape, were to me
More dear, both for themselves and for thy sake!

*   *   *

By R. J. Hutchings:

Landfalls of the Romantic Poets (James Brodie)

Idylls of Farringford—Alfred Tennyson (Brodie)

King of the Mystics—Robert Browning (Brodie)

Dickens on an Island (Brodie)

Island of Poetry—an Illustrated Anthology of Isle of
Wight Poetry (G. G. Saunders)

The Wordsworth Poetical Guide to the Lakes (Hunnyhill
Publications, Brighstone I.W.)

Young Algernon Swinburne—the Poet's Associations with the
Isle of Wight (Hunnyhill), with Dr. R. V. Turley

West Country Poems of Wordsworth & Coleridge (Hunnyhill
Publications, 1979)

Other Hunnyhill Publications:

Old Lakeland Photographs, from a collection of E. Alan Marsh,
1978

The Loss of the Mary Rose, by S. Horsey Sen.; first print 1844
Reprinted 1975. Second Impression 1978.

*   *   *

Published by *Hunnyhill Publications*,
Corner Cottage, Hunnyhill, Brighstone, Isle of Wight.
Printed by *Yelf Bros. Ltd.*, Newport, Isle of Wight